The **Essential** Buyer's Guide

HONDA

CBR600/ Hurricane

All models, 599cc, 1987 to 2010

Your marque expert:
Peter Henshaw

T0386687

VELOCE PUBLISHING
THE PUBLISHER OF FINE AUTOMOTIVE BOOKS

Also from Veloce –

www.veloce.co.uk

First published in July 2011 by Veloce Publishing Limited, Veloce House, Parkway Farm Business Park, Middle Farm Way, Poundbury, Dorchester, Dorset, DT1 3AR, England. Fax 01305 250479/ e-mail info@veloce.co.uk/web www.veloce.co.uk or www.velocebooks.com.

ISBN: 978-1-845843-09-0 UPC: 6-36847-04309-4

British Library Cataloguing in Publication Data – A catalogue record for this book is available from the British Library. Typesetting, design and page make-up all by Veloce Publishing Ltd on Apple Mac. Printed in India by Imprint Digital.

Compromise is sometimes seen as a dirty word, but the Honda CBR600 (Hurricane in the USA) takes it to a fine art. This is one of the most versatile motorcycles ever made: it's able to deliver adrenalin on a weekend blast, perform well on track days, and commute to work Monday to Friday, or even go touring. And it will do all of this equally well, reliably, and without fuss.

The CBR600 (Hurricane USA) is one of motorcycling's great all-rounders.

For many years, Honda's long-lived 600 was the best Supersports machine and the best seller all over the world. Over the years, it shed weight and gained power, while the top speed increased from 140mph to over 160mph.

Despite the performance potential (and later RR models are more committed sports bikes than the earlier F models), the CBR is a practical workhorse that can rack up high mileages with only routine maintenance. The F, in particular, is good day-to-day, with decent mirrors, a centre stand, grab rail, and comfy seat. As with all Hondas, the CBRs are well engineered, quality machines with very few foibles. Some say the bike lacks character compared with its more 'manic' 600cc rivals, but if that's a drawback, it's obviously one that thousands of owners can live with.

This book is a straightforward, practical guide to buying a secondhand CBR. It doesn't list all the correct colour combinations for each year, or delve into the minutiae of year-by-year changes (though we have provided a brief guide); there are books and websites that will supply all of that. But, hopefully, it will help you avoid the proverbial lemon because, as with any bike, there are some to be found.

The good news is that because the CBR600 has sold so well for so long, there

2010 CBR600 (foreground) ... as focused as its FireBlade stablemate.

Most CBR owners are happy with their bikes.

are many secondhand examples around, from the very affordable to the almost new. So, if you don't like the look of one, simply get back on the 'phone and make a booking to see another – there's plenty of choice. One thing to bear in mind is that the CBR600 family comprises two different bikes: the CBR600 F (1987-2006) – the consummate all-rounder – and the F-Sport and RR (2001-2010), more focused sports bikes that sacrifice some day-to-day practicality for ultimate performance. Either way, you should be able to find a good buy.

Thanks are due to Matt Saunders, at V&J Honda, to Honda UK, and Annice Collet at the VMCC Library. Also, to all those CBR owners who allowed me to use pictures of their bikes: Nigel Bishop, Steve Saffer, Rona Bell, Nigel Wild, and Claire Robins.

Essential Buyer's Guide™ currency
At the time of publication a BG unit of currency "●" equals approximately £1.00/US$1.63/Euro 1.12. Please adjust to suit current exchange rates.

Contents

1 Is it the right bike for you?
– marriage guidance

Tall and short riders
The CBR600 is a compact bike; the F has a riding position that will suit a wide range of shapes and sizes, but the smaller RR is a little cramped for six-foot plus riders.

Running costs
Varies a lot, depending on riding style and level of home maintenance. Ride the CBR600 hard, and you will pay the price in tyre, brake pad, and chain/sprocket life, yet it will always be cheaper to run than a big sports bike. Expect 40-45mpg from a carburettor bike (those up to 1998) in normal, mixed riding, up to 50mpg when treated more gently, and less than 40mpg ridden hard. Fuel injected bikes are thirstier.

Maintenance
Not very demanding, with a minor service at 4000, interim at 8000, and major (including valve clearances) at 16,000 miles. The minor and interim services are straightforward for most competent DIY mechanics. Consumables (brake pads, tyres, chain sprockets) also present no particular problems. Centre stand on CBR600F makes chain/tyre maintenance easy.

Usability
One of the CBR's strong points. The F will tour two-up, take you to work Monday-Friday, and still be a good sports bike waiting to break free at weekends.

Parts availability
Excellent. Just about everything, for every CBR back to 1987, is available from Honda dealers, though you will have to order, as they don't keep much in stock. Bike breakers are a good source of cheaper secondhand parts.

Parts costs
Routine service items – filters, brake pads and so on – are inexpensive, and in the normal run of things, that's all you'll need. If the bike needs major or

The CBR is great fun to ride (look at the grin!)

crash damage repairs, life can get expensive. But don't forget the bike breakers for secondhand parts: there's plenty of choice, but be satisfied that the part you're paying for is from a reputable seller and in good condition.

Insurance group
Highish: UK Group 14 for the CBR600F, UK Group 15 for the RR – though it won't cost any more to insure than other 600cc sports bikes. Riders aged under 30 will pay a premium, as will those with a poor insurance record.

Investment potential
Virtually zero, as the CBR has always sold well over its 20-year plus production run, and there lots of them still around. In the future, the F-Sport might have some investment potential, as it was only sold for three years. Bikes in racing team colours (eg: Movistar) will be more sought after.

Foibles
Very few. Camchain tensioner and regulator/rectifier are the only known weak spots.

Plus points
All-round versatility, combining exciting performance with everyday practicality. Good handling, easy to ride. The RR is biased more towards performance, the F towards all round use.

Minus points
Not everyone gets on with the riding position, and some say that the CBR600 is bland.

Alternatives
You're spoilt for choice. Equivalent 600cc sports bikes are; Yamaha R6, Suzuki GSX-R600, Kawasaki ZX-6R, or Triumph's TT600/Daytona 650 and 675. If you don't fancy the sports bike image, Honda's own CBR600-engined Hornet and Yamaha's Fazer are practical naked bikes.

2 Cost considerations
– affordable, or a money pit?

The CBR600 can be quite a cheap bike to run, given some home maintenance, and (if it's an older bike ridden by a 40-plus rider) reasonable insurance costs. Tyres can last very well, up to 10,000 miles rear and over 20,000 front, though far less with a hard rider. Ditto with brake pads – maybe 8000 miles with hard use, or up to 25,000 if used more gently. Service costs at a Honda dealer are around ◉x150 for the 4000 mile service, ◉x200 for the 8000 mile, and up to ◉x400 for the 16,000 mile, including a valve clearance check. Spares prices, below, are from a Honda specialist, a mix of genuine Honda and pattern parts.

Air filter element ◉x21
Battery ◉x30
Brake disc (one) ◉x125
Brake lever ◉x18
Brake pads (front set) ◉x32
Camchain tensioner ◉x45
Clutch pressure plate ◉x18
Clutch cable ◉x12
Chain and sprocket kit ◉x99
Exhaust downpipes ◉x199
Exhaust silencer ◉x228
Fairing lower ◉x236
Fairing top ◉x458
Fork seal set (per leg) ◉x13.50
Ignition coil/plug cap (ea) ◉x35

Mirror ◉x42
Oil filter ◉x6
Regulator/rectifier ◉x85
Starter solenoid ◉x49
Tyre (front) ◉x70
Tyre (rear) ◉x110
Wiring harness ◉x75

These bikes don't cost an arm and leg to run.

They're easy on tyres, unless you're a hard rider.

3 Living with a CBR600
– will you get along together?

Some motorcycles, especially sports bikes, demand a degree of commitment from the owner. They can be a literal pain in the backside (or wrists, neck, or shoulders) after half an hour on the road. They might need rigorous, specialist maintenance, or be very quick to corrode. Or they might be superb on track days, but awkward and intractable in town.

All the bikes are easy to live with, but the RR (this is a 2010) is less of an all-rounder than the F.

The CBR600 isn't one of those. In fact, it's probably one of the easiest sports bikes to live with. As such, it's the ideal first sports bike for those who have never taken the plunge before. The riding position of the CBR600 F in particular (sold up to 2006) is moderate by sports bike standards, with higher bars and lower footrests than, say, an R6 or GSX-R600.

It's more comfortable at low speeds, and with the best will in the world, we all spend some time in town or in heavy traffic. The same goes for the pillion, with a decent-sized seat and even a grab rail (quite unusual on a sports bike). If you're intending to ride two-up for more than short hops, then it's the sports bike to have. The RR (2003 on) and F-Sport (2001-03) are less comfy and more committed, with lower bars, higher footrests, and skimpier, separate seats for rider and pillion. But they're still relatively comfy by sports bike standards, especially at higher speeds.

That's why it's often said that CBR owners are as likely to use their bikes for touring and commuting as for weekend blasts and trackdays, and several of the bikes pictured in this book do just that. If you want something more focused for fast road riding and track days, an R6 might be a better bet, but as a consummate all-rounder, a 'do it all' sort of bike, the CBR is hard to beat.

This relative comfort is complemented by very accessible performance. Although it's true the CBR has little power at low to medium revs, that doesn't mean it's difficult to ride – one just gets used to changing down a gear or two before overtaking. A CBR doesn't have the effortless performance of a one-litre superbike, like its FireBlade stablemate, but that does have an upside: bigger sports bikes are great fun to ride, but can be frighteningly fast in the wrong circumstances. The CBR, like any of the sports 600s, is fast enough to be fun (you can't argue with a 140-160mph top speed) but you are less likely to lose your licence (or worse) on one. And, at the other end of the speed range, it's quiet and tractable, happy to trundle through town at 3000rpm or less. The only thing that detracts from in-town riding is a bit of slack in the drive train and a notchy gearchange, especially on older bikes.

Comfy dual seat and grab rail makes the F especially good two-up.

Today, 600cc sports bikes are seen as relatively modest machines, but they still offer supercar acceleration (as long as you're in the right gear) and the sheer adrenalin buzz of a five-figure red line. Despite this, the CBR doesn't have a demanding maintenance schedule. This is a Honda after all, a quality bike designed to give reliable high-performance as long as it's properly maintained. There's a minor service (oil, filter plus checks) at 4000 miles, which, for some riders, will mean once a year, or every few months for the commuters. An intermediate service comes at 8000 miles, and a major at 16,000, which includes a valve clearance check. From 2006, iridium sparkplugs meant the plug change time was doubled to 24,000 miles.

Of course, as with any bike, you will need to keep an eye on consumables between services – chain, sprockets, brake pads, and tyres. The life expectancy of all these things is hugely dependent on riding style – do a lot of track days and you'll wear out tyres and pads far more quickly than a commuter. Wheelies can be addictive, but they also give the chain and sprockets a hard time. But the CBR will be far less hungry than a one-litre sports bike, and as the CBR is the most popular bike in its class, spares couldn't be easier to get hold of.

Security is an issue with any bike, and Honda fitted a decent steering lock to the CBR, with the HISS immobiliser system from 1999. But, sadly, the CBR600 is quite stealable, thanks to its light weight and ready saleability. And because there are so many around, it's relatively easy to give one a false identity, or break it up for spares. When looking at a bike, make a point of checking that the VIN on the frame corresponds with that on the documentation, and use a HPI check on the bike's history. If you do buy it, keep the bike safe with your own security measures, whether at home or out and about.

We've referred to several advantages the CBR has over a big sports bike, and there's one more: insurance. It will always be cheaper to insure than a FireBlade of similar value, though younger riders or those with a poor riding record (or worse still, both) will literally pay a heavy premium. Insurance companies prefer middle-aged riders with a clean licence.

CBRs are bought and ridden by riders of all ages. There aren't many machines with such a wide appeal, and it's easy to see why: a CBR is fast, yet easy to live with, equally capable of touring or commuting (in F form), as well as track days, and not too demanding in maintenance and running costs. It's a true all-rounder.

4 Relative values
– which model for you?

See chapter 12 for value assessment. This chapter shows, in percentage terms, the value of individual models in good condition, and looks at the strengths and weaknesses of each model, so that you can decide which is best for you. Generally, the CBR became more and more sporting as the years went by, and we've broken it down into five categories: the original CBR (1987-90), the F2/F3 (last of the steel-framed bikes), the F4 (alloy frame from 1999, with fuel-injection from 2001), the F-Sport, and RR (a very different and more sharply focused sports bike). Note that the CBR600 has been badged as the Honda Hurricane for the USA market.

Range availability

CBR600 F1

1987	F-H	83bhp
1988	F-J	83bhp
1989	F-K	93bhp
1990	F-L	93bhp

CBR600 F2

1991	F-M	99bhp
1992	F-N	99bhp
1993	F-P	99bhp
1994	F-R	99bhp

CBR600 F3

1995	F-S	100bhp
1996	F-T	100bhp
1997	F-V	105bhp
1998	F-W	105bhp

CBR600 F4

1999	F-X	110bhp
2000	F-Y	110bhp

2001	F-1	109bhp
2002	F-2	111bhp
2003	F-3	110bhp
2004	F-4	110bhp
2005	F-5	110bhp
2006	F-6	110bhp

CBR600 F-Sport

2001	FS-1	110bhp
2002	FS-2	110bhp
2003	FS-3	110bhp

CBR600 RR

2003	RR-3	117bhp
2004	RR-4	117bhp
2005	RR-5	117bhp
2006	RR-6	117bhp
2007	RR-7	118bhp
2008	RR-8	118bhp
2009	RR-9	118bhp
2010	RR-A	120bhp

CBR600 F1 (FH-FL, 1987-90)

Launched to great acclaim in 1987, the original CBR600 made a huge impact. Here was a reasonably compact, lightweight sports bike of just 600cc, with 83bhp and a top speed of 140mph. It had the best handling and best brakes in its class, yet it was still easy and comfortable to ride, able to carry a passenger and luggage. For many riders, a Yamaha FZR was too flighty and a Suzuki GSX600F too much of a tourer, making a CBR the ultimate compromise. It was badged as the Honda Hurricane in the USA.

There were minor changes to the FJ model in 1988, while the '89 FK had a significant power boost to 93bhp, thanks to a higher compression, larger carbs, and different valve timing. Upper midrange got a boost too, and top speed increased to 145mph. The rear shock acquired useful rebound damping adjustment, enabling the earlier bike's tendency to bounce to be dialled out. It also had more powerful

Some original early CBRs are still used day to day, like this one.

The earliest model is still the cheapest to buy.

brakes, and was the first bike with a CBR badge on the tank. In 1990, the bike was unchanged, apart from the colour choice.

These early series CBRs don't come up for sale very often. Plenty were sold, but they will be over 20 years old now – plenty of time to have been crashed, irretrievably broken down, or simply slotted into the back of a garage and forgotten about. The good news is that there's no price premium, so if you can find one, it should be the cheapest route to CBR ownership. Their age shows in the 2-pot Nissin brakes, which are fine for the road, but soft by modern standards, and marginal for a track day. The 1987-88 rear shock can be bouncy and the gearchange is notchy, with transmission slack at low speeds.

Pros: The original, which is an attraction in itself. Fast, but comfortable and easy to ride (which applies to all CBR600 Fs).

Cons: Over 20 years old. Brakes not the best. These aren't collectors' bikes, so you're unlikely to find one in pristine or restored condition.

CBR600 F1 – 31%

CBR600 F2 (FM-FR, 1991-94), CBR600 F3 (FS-FW, 1995-98)

The success of the first CBR600 saw competition in this market sector hot up considerably, and by 1990 the Honda had been overtaken by the Yamaha FZR on the track, and the Kawasaki ZZR600 on the road.

So, for 1991, Honda gave it a complete overhaul. First, the new F2 looked quite

Nicely kept 1991 CBR with topbox and aftermarket silencer.

1993 CBR was more of a sports bike.

1997 F, one of the last steel-framed CBRs.

different, with a higher seat and lower fairing. The engine had a bigger bore and shorter stroke, allowing higher revs and more power, now up to 99bhp. Carburettors went from 32mm to 34.5mm and there was an all-new 4-2-1 exhaust. The frame was still steel tubing (alloy was years away), but a new design with steeper steering head angle (from 26° to 25°), plus beefier 41mm forks and six-spoke wheels. In short, it was a better sports bike, while losing none of its touring/commuting abilities. Some minor changes to the F2 followed, with stepless rebound damping adjustment for the forks in 1993 and an air intake below the headlight for '94.

The debut of the F3, in '95, saw more radical changes. It kept the steel frame when most rivals were going down the alloy beam route, but it did add ram air induction and fully adjustable suspension. The ram air was said to improve engine responsiveness, even at low speeds, and power was up slightly, thanks to an increased compression ratio (now 12:1) and reduced internal friction with new pistons, while the flat-slide carburettors were now 36mm. Cooling was bolstered with a curved radiator and bigger oil cooler, while the exhaust downpipes were interconnected between cylinders 1 and 2, and 3 and 4, boosting midrange. The gearchange was made slightly smoother.

Chassis-wise, there was now rebound damping for the forks (adjuster on the fork top) and the rear wheel was widened from 4.5in to 5in, to allow the fitting of fatter tyres. The brakes were upgraded, too, with bigger 296mm floating front discs (though still with two-pot calipers).

It says much for the CBR's basic design that, apart from the 1995 revamp, the 1991 FM was substantially the same as the '98 FW. It's the classic all-rounder CBR600 F, as distinct from the later alloy-framed Fs – and even more so from the RR. As such, it's acceptably fast and handles well, but still has that big dual seat and practical touches like a centre stand, passenger grab rail, and underseat storage.

Pros: All the classic CBR virtues, but with a wider choice as more bikes are available. Later bikes have fully adjustable suspension.

Cons: Overtaken by contemporary sports bikes in handling and braking.

CBR600 F2 – 44%
CBR600 F3 – 60%

CBR600 F4 (FX-FY, 1999-2000), F4i (F-1-F-6, 2001-06)

The F4 marked a milestone in the CBR story, when the faithful steel frame was finally ditched in favour of an alloy beam frame. The result was a bike 15kg lighter, handled better, and was as fast as a Yamaha R6, but more comfortable and cheaper to insure. Although most of the changes were performance related, the F4 CBR did come with Honda's HISS immobiliser system, and kept the trademark centre stand.

The new frame had sharper geometry, which meant a friskier bike that was liable to flap its bars at high speed on bumpy roads (many bikes have an aftermarket steering damper to cure this).

2001 bike on offer at a dealer, now with alloy frame.

As well as the new frame, the engine had a shorter stroke and larger valves, to intensify the pursuit of higher revs and more power. Some torque was lost, but the new engine now revved happily to 12,700rpm and was smoother, though some bikes suffered from a flatspot at 5000rpm. A potentially more serious problem concerned the camshaft holding caps, which could move sideways when torqued down, pinching the cam bearings and starving them of oil. It only appeared to affect bikes that had been raced. There was no recall, but Honda introduced a new torque procedure that cured it.

The F4 brakes were uprated too, using FireBlade parts, and the F4 marked a real turning point, with an increasing emphasis on the sports bike side of the CBR's nature. It doesn't have quite such a good reputation for reliability as the F1-F3, and it's less comfortable.

Another milestone arrived in 2001, with fuel-injection. This was Honda's PGM-FI system, which boosted power by 5bhp and top speed to 165mph. Honda claimed more precise fuel metering over a wider rpm, giving better throttle response. It certainly impressed the road testers, who found the injection system free of glitches,

Twin headlights and ram air intakes on this 2001 machine.

with a smooth on/off throttle transition. But it was thirstier, with mpg into the mid-30s.

Not all of the extra power was down to the injection. Revised engine internals allowed a higher 14,200rpm rev limit; lower overall gearing (not only in fifth and sixth) improved acceleration, too. The 2001-on injected bike had still sharper styling and the frame benefitted from a stiffer headstock and stronger swingarm. Wheelbase was reduced by 5mm and unsprung weight cut, thanks to lighter wheels and brake caliper carrier.

The 2001 fuel-injection makeover was the F's last big change. From 2003 it was increasingly in the shadow of the RR (see below), reflecting a 600cc Supersports market that was more interested in hard-edged sports bikes than all-round versatility. But, the F did continue until 2006, largely unchanged. For 2011 (outside the scope of this book), Honda announced that the CBR600 F would return using Hornet running gear.

Pros: Faster, lighter, and better handling than the steel-framed CBRs, more suitable for track days. Fuel-injection works very well. Plenty of choice secondhand.

Cons: Less comfortable than the F1-F3, and some say less reliable. Injected bikes use more fuel.

CBR600 F4 – 80%
CBR600 F4i – 130%

CBR600 F-Sport (FS1, 2 and 3, 2001-03)

Despite the alloy frame and fuel-injection, the CBR F was still getting left behind by more hard-edged rivals, especially in racing. There was speculation that Honda would launch a real 'racer-with-lights' to meet the challenge, but when the F-Sport

The relatively rare F-Sport: the two-piece seat is an identifier.

was launched in 2001, it proved to be nothing of the sort. In fact, it was more of a stepping stone between the F and the forthcoming RR.

It's easily differentiated from the F, with a sleeker fairing, black (not silver) frame, and stepped seat, though the suspension and frame geometry were unchanged. Under the skin, however, there were a few detail changes, aimed at making the Sport an easier proposition to upgrade as a true racer.

Power increased, very slightly, thanks to a re-profiled cam, stronger valve springs, and 15,750rpm limit. An extra clutch plate was added and the centre stand, grab rail, and one-piece seat all ditched to save weight.

Despite the changes, this was still very much a CBR, with highish bars and low footpegs by sports bike standards. The suspension, too, was considered a little soft for fast track days, while the low pegs limited ground clearance. In its first year, the Sport came in SP-1 inspired colours of red and black, and in '02 the options were silver, white, red, or yellow (the latter a Valentino Rossi replica). ·

It may have disappointed some, but the Sport was popular, easy to hop on and ride with confidence, and the race version bagged Honda the World Supersport Championship in 2002.

Pros: As easy to ride as the F, but looks sportier. Rarity value, with relatively short production run.

Cons: Many were bought by club racers, so look for the tell-tale signs (dinged wheels, worn head races, and replacement body panels). Really no faster or better handling than the F.

CBR600 F-Sport – 109%

CBR600 RR (RR3-RR9, RRA, 2003-10)

Honda wanted to grab back its dominance of the 600 Supersport class, and the Sport was, arguably, just a holding operation until the CBR600 RR was ready. The RR represented a complete change of philosophy, being much more sports focused than any of its predecessors.

At its launch in 2003, much was made by Honda of the RR's resemblance to the RCV211V, the company's MotoGP racer. That was overplayed, but there were certainly similarities, the most obvious being the underseat exhaust. The styling was very similar, and they also shared the Unit Pro Link rear end, which played a central role in the design philosophy of mass centralisation. In Unit Pro Link, the suspension linkage was attached to the swingarm instead of the frame, preventing suspension loads being fed to the headstock. This set up was very compact, hiding the shock

The RR (2010 shown) was quite different to earlier CBRs.

Radial-mounted calipers and other changes brought powerful, sensitive braking.

Only the RR had an underseat exhaust.

and liberating space underneath the seat. Honda took advantage of this by moving the fuel tank to beneath the seat, furthering the aim of keeping all weight as central as possible.

With the same goal, the CBR's traditional riding position was transformed, with lower bars and higher footrests moving the rider's weight further forward. The frame was designed to flex under cornering forces, just like the Moto GP racer (though in a different way), and the forks were upgraded to 45mm Showas. Power delivery was improved with an extra set of injectors in the airbox, giving an initial air/fuel mix and denser charge.

The RR feels quite different to any CBR600 F. The whole bike was physically smaller, and the rider sits on top of the bike rather than in it. Because it's small, the RR can feel cramped for tall riders. Road testers raved about the bike, since handling and braking were now right at the top of the class, and thought to be a reasonable trade off for some of the old CBR's comfort and weather protection. The body panels were thinner and more flimsy than the F's, to save weight.

Despite the extra power and higher revs, the power delivery isn't much more peaky, and this is still a civilised and easy bike to ride. The RR does lack some of the F's convenience features, such as underseat storage and a centre stand, and the mirrors are '50% elbow view,' according to one road test, while pillions are relegated to a tiny perch – par for the course on a modern sports bike. On the other hand, you still have bungee hooks, a clock, fuel gauge, and HISS immobiliser.

There have been two major updates to the RR, the first, in 2005, concentrated on the cycle parts and saving yet more weight. Five kilos lighter than the '04 bike, the '05 also had inverted forks, radial front brake calipers, and a 5mm longer swingarm. The frame had different wall thicknesses – thicker around the headstock and swingarm pivot, thinner in non-crucial areas, to save weight, and there were lighter pistons, a smoother power delivery, and slightly more torque.

In 2007, the RR was completely re-engineered with a new engine and frame. The engine was 2kg lighter, revved 500rpm higher, had a stronger midrange, and produced 118bhp. The wheelbase was reduced to 1375mm and the frame was lighter, with a beefed up headstock incorporating the ram air duct. A welcome addition was the electronic steering damper from the FireBlade. This was speed sensitive, linked to the ECU, so that steering was undamped at low speeds, keeping it light in town. The CBR was now thought to be the best looking 600 Supersport, and was the best seller once again.

In 2009, linked ABS brakes were a new option, big news for a sports bike. It was a very advanced electronic system that worked via the lever or pedal; apply either one, and the system would automatically apportion front/rear braking according to the conditions. It was considered excellent, unobtrusive in normal riding, and backed up by an anti-lock that allowed the bike to stop safely in deep gravel. The 2009 RR also had slightly more midrange power.

Pros: Excellent handling and braking, stunning performance, smooth power delivery. Sold well, so plenty to choose from secondhand.

Cons: Less comfortable than the F (especially for pillions), less room for tall riders, less of an all-rounder.

CBR600 RR – 170%

Alternatives
Plenty. The most obvious are the equivalent Supersport 600s – Suzuki GSX-R, Yamaha YZR and R6, Kawasaki ZX6-R, Triumph TT600 Daytona 650 and 675. Kawasaki's ZZR600 is a good alternative to the early CBR. Some of these alternatives are faster, some better handling, but none has the all-round abilities of the Honda. If you fancy an Italian bike, there's the Ducati 748, but it's far from the comfort and convenience of a CBR. If you like the all-rounder character of the early

bike, but the RR is too focused, have a look at Honda's Hornet and CBF600, both powered by de-tuned CBR engines, with a more relaxed riding position and added comfort.

The Hornet offers some of the CBR's riding experience, but with a more upright position.

5 Before you view
– be well informed

To avoid a wasted journey, and the disappointment of finding that the bike does not match your expectations, it will help if you're very clear about what questions you want to ask before you pick up the phone. Some of these points might appear basic, but when you're excited about the prospect of buying your dream bike, it's amazing how some of the most obvious things slip the mind. Also check the current values of the model in which you are interested in the classified ads.

Where is the bike?
Is it going to be worth travelling to the next county/state, or even across a border? A locally advertised machine, although it may not sound very interesting, can add to your knowledge for very little effort, so make a visit – it might even be in better condition than expected.

Dealer or private sale?
Establish early on if the bike is being sold by its owner or by a trader. A private owner should have all the history, so don't be afraid to ask detailed questions. A dealer may have more limited knowledge of the bike's history, but should have some documentation. A dealer may offer a warranty/guarantee (ask for a printed copy).

Cost of collection and delivery?
A dealer may well be used to quoting for delivery. A private owner may agree to meet you halfway, but only agree to this after you have seen the bike at the vendor's address to validate the documents. Conversely, you could meet halfway and agree the sale, but insist on meeting at the vendor's address for the handover.

View – when and where?
It is always preferable to view at the vendor's home or business premises. In the case of a private sale, the bike's documentation should tally with the vendor's name and address. Arrange to view only in daylight, and avoid a wet day – the vendor may be reluctant to let you take a test ride if it's wet.

Reason for sale?
Do make it one of the first questions. Why is the bike being sold and how long has it been with the current owner? How many previous owners?

Condition?
Ask for an honest appraisal of the bike's condition. Ask specifically about some of the check items described in chapter 8.

All original specification?
CBR owners love to fit accessories, and old bikes especially are unlikely to have the original silencer. Braided brake hoses are a good sign, and many owners fit things like bellypans and tinted screens. If the original screen, silencer etc comes as part of the deal, so much the better. If an older bike is completely original, then it's quite a find, though it won't make a huge difference to the value.

Matching data/legal ownership?
Does the VIN and licence plate match the official registration document? Is the owner's name and address recorded in the official registration documents?

For those countries that require an annual test of roadworthiness, does the bike have a document showing it complies (an MoT certificate in the UK, which can be verified on 0845 600 5977)?

Does the bike carry a current road fund license/licence plate tag? No CBR600 is old enough to qualify for tax exempt status in the UK.

Does the vendor own the bike outright? Money might be owed to a finance company or bank: the bike could even be stolen. Several organisations will supply the data on ownership, based on the bike's licence plate number, for a fee. Such companies can often also tell you whether the bike has been 'written-off' by an insurance company. In the UK these organisations can supply vehicle data:

HPI – 01722 422 422 – www.hpicheck.com
AA – 0870 600 0836 – www.theaa.com
RAC – 0870 533 3660 – www.rac.co.uk
Other countries will have similar organisations.

Insurance
Check with your existing insurer before setting out – your current policy might not cover you if you do buy the bike and decide to ride it home.

How you can pay?
A cheque/check will take several days to clear and the seller may prefer to sell to a cash buyer. However, a banker's draft (a cheque issued by a bank) is as good as cash, but safer, so contact your own bank and become familiar with the formalities that are necessary to obtain one.

Buying at auction?
If the intention is to buy at auction see chapter 10 for further advice.

Professional vehicle check (mechanical examination)
In the UK, the AA and RAC no longer perform used motorcycle checks. A Honda dealer or independent specialist may be willing to check a bike over for a fee, but you'll need to get the owner's permission first.

6 Inspection equipment
– these items will really help

Before you rush out of the door, gather together a few items that will help as you work your way around the bike.

This book
This book is designed to be your guide at every step, so take it along and use the check boxes in chapter 9 to help you assess each area of the bike. Don't be afraid to let the seller see you using it.

Reading glasses (if you need them for close work)
Take your reading glasses if you need them to read documents and make close up inspections.

Overalls
Be prepared to get dirty. Take along a pair of overalls, if you have them.

Digital camera
A digital camera is handy so that later you can study some areas of the bike more closely. Take a picture of any part of the bike that causes you concern, and seek an expert opinion.

Paddock stand
A paddock stand is especially useful if the bike doesn't have a centre stand, and many owners will already have one. By propping up either end of the bike, it makes checking of tyres, chain, sprockets and wheel bearings far easier.

A friend, preferably a knowledgeable enthusiast
Ideally, have a friend or knowledgeable enthusiast come along with you to see the bike – a second opinion is always worth having.

7 Ten minute evaluation
– walk away or stay?

Documentation

If the seller claims to be the bike's owner, make sure he/she really is by checking the registration document, which in the UK is listed on theV5C. The person listed on the V5 isn't necessarily the legal owner, but their details should match those of whoever is selling the bike. Also, use the V5C to check the VIN.

You can learn quite a lot in 10 minutes.

An annual roadworthiness certificate – the 'MoT' in the UK – is handy proof that the bike was roadworthy when tested. A whole sheaf of them gives evidence of the bike's history – when it was actively being used, and what the mileage was. The more of these come with the bike, the better. Ask for any service history as well – routine servicing, repairs and recalls.

VIN Number

Does the VIN (Vehicle Identification Number) tally with that on the documentation? The number is either stamped on the right-hand side of the headstock, or marked on a plate fixed to the right-hand side of the frame, just in front of the fuel tank. Do the numbers look original, not tampered with? UK buyers should check the white sticker behind the VIN plate/number (see page 25) to confirm that the bike is UK spec, not a parallel import.

The VIN is an important check point.

If the numbers don't tally, the bike could have been built from stolen parts. If the owner can't come up with a convincing explanation, walk away – there are plenty of legitimate CBRs to choose from.

General condition

With the bike outside and in good light, put it on the centre stand, if there is one, and take a good, slow walk around it. If it's claimed to be restored, and has a nice shiny tank and engine cases, look more closely – how far does the 'restored' finish go? Are the

Take a good long look around the bike.

nooks and crannies behind the gearbox as spotless as the fuel tank? If not, the bike may have been given a quick smarten up to sell. A generally faded look all over isn't necessarily a bad thing – it suggests a machine that hasn't been restored, and isn't trying to pretend that it has.

The most crucial thing to look for on any CBR is evidence of crash damage, and whether it's been raced. Is the bodywork unmarked or suspiciously new, on an otherwise tatty bike? When a bike does hit the deck, the same things suffer almost every time, so take a good look at the silencer, footrests, mirrors, indicators, levers, and bar ends for signs of trips down the road. Plastic bodywork protectors can be bent or scratched (though they're very easy to replace). Scraped engines or clutch cases (or even worse, holed cases, hastily patched up with resin) are confirmation of a hard life. Lockwired bolts and chipped wheel rims are evidence of a racing career.

Engine/suspension/tyres

Check the engine oil – via a dipstick on early bikes, or a window in the crankcase on later models – both on the right-hand side of the engine. Is it at the correct level? No metal particles floating around? Start the engine. It should fire up promptly and rev crisp and clean. Blip the throttle and watch for blue smoke, a sign of top end wear. Listen to the engine: a rattle at idle could be a problem with the camchain tensioner, and any knocks or rumbles are signs of serious camshaft or bearing wear.

Tyres and chain are other indicators of whether the owner is a caring type or not. Are the tyres worn right round to the sidewalls, or just in the centre? Well worn rubber is a good bargaining counter. Now look at the chain – is it properly adjusted and nicely lubed? Is the rear sprocket in good condition? If not, take the cost of replacements into account.

Check the front forks for oil leaks, and with the bike on its centre stand or propped up, check them for play by grasping the bottom of the legs and trying to rock them back and forth. With the front wheel back on the ground, and the front brake on, pump the forks up and down – they should move smoothly and without squeaks or rattles.

Sit on the bike and check the rear suspension – as with the forks, the shock should move smoothly and quietly. If it feels oversoft, then it could need replacing.

Tyres are easy to check ... but they won't be like this one!

The state of nuts, bolts, and other fasteners is a good indication of previous owner attitudes. Chewed up or rounded off fixings are signs of a neglectful or ham-fisted owner – apart from a few marks on the surrounding bodywork, this one's fine.

Unlike many other sports bikes, some CBR600s get used all year round, often every day, so you might well find a 50,000 mile plus bike. As long as it's been properly maintained, that shouldn't be a problem, as CBRs are well able to cope with high mileages (though a 50,000-mile bike will always be worth less than a 20,000-mile).

Another must-see check – the VIN. Check that the number doesn't look tampered with, and that it matches the documentation.

Is there any evidence of crash damage? This scraped cover was caused by a minor slide down the road. Check the bodywork, footrests, bar ends, mirrors, silencer, and steering stops.

Disc thickness is another good indication of owner care – worn discs are relatively easy to replace, but not cheap. New discs on an old bike are a good sign. This is what a new disc will look like.

9 Serious evaluation
– 30 minutes for years of enjoyment

Score each section using the boxes as follows:
4 = excellent; 3 = good; 2 = average; 1 = poor. The totting up procedure is detailed at the end of the chapter. Be realistic in your marking!

VIN number

The VIN (Vehicle Identification Number) is mentioned several times in this book, and with good reason: there's no better way to check that a bike is bona fide. The engine number is, like the engine itself, hidden behind the fairing, so unless the seller is happy for you to remove bodywork, it won't be possible to check this.

Fortunately, the VIN is easy to find, either stamped onto the right-hand side of the headstock, or on a plate fixed to the frame just in front of the fuel tank, again on the right-hand side.

The VIN number is either stamped on the headstock ...

... or on a plate fixed to the frame.

Have a good look at the numbers. Do they look as if they've been tampered with? If so, walk away. The quickest way to change a stolen bike's identity is to try and change the numbers.

Check the VIN against that on the documentation – if it's not identical, then the bike isn't what the seller says it is. If the seller says that the bike has had a replacement frame, well, maybe it has, but the registration authorities must have been informed and the documentation changed to suit.

For buyers in the UK, there's one other thing to check on the VIN. In the late 1990s, new bike prices in Britain were significantly higher than those in some other parts of Europe. 'Parallel imports' were bikes shipped to the UK from mainland Europe and sold at a lower price than the official imports sold by Honda UK. These weren't always to UK specification – the differences are small (look for a km/h speedo and right-hand dipping headlight) but a non-UK spec bike is generally worth less than an official one. CBRs from 1996-98 were especially affected. Another check is to look for a white sticker on the frame, behind the headstock: on a UK-spec bike, this will display an 'E' and a number – other markets had a different letter.

The bottom line is; if in doubt, walk away. There are lots of secondhand CBR600s around, and most of them have nothing serious to hide.

Paintwork and decals are expensive to put right – these are perfect.

Even Honda alloy will eventually corrode.

Paint/alloy

Honda's paint finish is good, but, as on any bike, it is susceptible to neglect. The fuel tank may have become worn by crouching riders, but many owners add stick-on pads to prevent this.

Take a look at the fairing sides for scratch damage; a gentle slide down the road may have left the bodywork intact, but made a real mess of the paintwork or decals. Fairing colour schemes are a big part of any CBR's appeal, especially those with race replica colours. Fairings can be repainted and decals replaced, but it all takes time and money, so again, damage here should be reflected in the price.

There's plenty of alloy on a CBR. As with the paintwork, Honda's finish is pretty good quality, but the bike only needs to be left unwashed after a couple of salty rides for corrosion to take hold – plating comes off alloy and steel parts rust. This affects all bikes, though obviously the older they are the more they are likely to have suffered, and it takes a meticulous owner to have washed the bike after every winter ride. On bikes with painted steel swingarms, watch for the paint flaking and allowing rust to take hold around the chain adjusters.

Check the engine cases and lower fork legs for peeling or bubbling lacquer, and all alloy parts for corrosion. None of this affects how the bike runs, but it looks unsightly and has an affect on value, if only because some CBR600s have been summer use-only bikes, and haven't suffered from winter corrosion. If you do decide to ignore the corrosion and bag yourself a bargain, don't forget that it will be more difficult to sell-on.

Bodywork

In one respect, buying a secondhand bike is far easier than purchasing a used car – there's far less bodywork to worry about. The quality of Honda's plastic is pretty good, though it will still suffer if the bike has been dropped. The panels should be secure, and check that the fasteners aren't loose, damaged, or missing.

Many owners fit plastic bodywork protectors (bungs), which do a good job if the bike does go down: check these aren't scraped or bent. If they are overtightened, they can crack the castings they're bolted to.

Look for blemishes around fasteners.

Bodywork protectors do a good job, but check they're not bent.

If the fairing is cracked or badly scraped, new Honda replacements aren't cheap, though most are available, as are the correct decals. Bike breakers are a good source of secondhand panels, of which there's a reasonable supply,

So, cracked plastic is no reason to reject a bike, as long as the damage is reflected in the price, and you're prepared to search for and fit a replacement. It may also need repainting to match the rest of the bike. One alternative to a breaker is aftermarket bodywork, cheaper than Honda's own.

Either way, a new looking fairing on an otherwise shabby bike suggests it has been crashed. A minority of CBRs have had a chequered career in club racing, and racers sometimes fit cheap panels to save the originals. Track day use is far more common ... and so is the ensuing damage!

Badges/decals

All badges and graphics are stick-on, and according to at least one Honda dealer, all are available as new spares.

This is one of the simpler decals.

Decal on a 2010 RR – they actually last very well unless damaged.

But as ever, if it's damaged on the bike you're looking at, that's another good lever to get the price down. Peeling off old graphics, and getting new ones in the right place without creases or bubbles, is never as straightforward as it seems.

Seat

A generous dual-seat features on all CBR600 Fs, with separate (and skimpier) rider/pillion perches on the F-Sport and RR. As with any seat, check for splits and tears: not only does this look tatty, but it allows rain water in,

Check rider and passenger seats for splits and tears ...

... or a severe case of ingrained dirt.

which the foam padding soaks up ... and never fully dries out. Recovering is the only answer; something which any motorcycle seat specialist can do, and as these aren't big items, it shouldn't cost much either. The pillion seat on the F-Sport and RR are unlikely to have seen much use!

Footrests

Worn footrests are a good indicator of mileage, though, of course, they are quite easy and cheap to replace; if they're noticeably newer and shinier than the rest of the bike, it's a sure sign that they have been. Check the footrest protectors (otherwise known as 'hero blob') underneath the rests; if they are

Have the footrest hero blobs ever touched tarmac ... ?

... and are the rubbers worn?

scraped, it's a sign of a hard, enthusiastic rider – though that's not necessarily a bad thing. Don't forget the pillion rests, too, for a general check.

Frame

Frame condition is vital to the safety and performance of any bike: its integrity affects the handling, and it can sustain quite serious damage which won't be immediately obvious. It might even be bad enough to write-off the bike, as any sort of problem here usually means replacing the whole frame – that's sometimes more than the entire bike is worth.

The good news is that all CBR frames are well made and very strong, built to take the sort of abuse that sports bikes can suffer. Your difficulty as a buyer is that it's not easy to examine every inch of the frame. What you can do is use a straight edge to check that the wheels are in line (though a problem here could simply be a misaligned rear wheel) and the visible parts of the main frame spars for dents (watch for strategically placed carbon fibre strips stuck on to hide them). With the handlebars on full lock, have a look at the headstock; after the forks, this takes the brunt of any head-on collision, so check for any signs of damage. Check the steering stops, the little lugs that limit handlebar movement. If they are damaged, that's a sign of a crash – they may even have snapped off altogether.

On early bikes, the side panels are relatively easy to remove, but the seat needs to be unbolted. The seller may or may not be willing to let you take the seat off to examine the frame underneath. If not, don't worry too much – the crucial points are the headstock, wheel alignment, and how the bike rides on the road.

Finally, when out on the test ride (see below) check that the bike runs in a straight line (though, again, veering to one side could simply be poor rear wheel alignment) and responds well to steering input.

Steel frames rust, though there's no structural problem here.

Check alloy frame spars for dents and dings.

Side stand should be secure.

Does the centre stand (F models only) work smoothly?

Stands

The CBR600 F is unique among sports bikes in having a centre stand. This adds weight and reduces ground clearance, but the ability to hold the rear wheel off the ground makes chain lubrication and wheel removal far easier. It's also a help when checking a secondhand machine.

If you come across a 1987 CBR (and not many have survived), the centre stand had a weak pivot tube and could collapse. Whatever the year, check that the stand works smoothly and retracts promptly; a lazy spring means it could flap around over bumps, and some centre stands are so seldom used they seize up.

The side stand is sturdy enough, but do check that it springs back properly (you don't want a tired spring allowing it to drop onto the road while riding) and that it's firm on its bearing (which cannot be lubed and will eventually wear out).

The stand has a cut-out to switch off the engine if the stand is operated while the engine's running. To check this is working, sit on the bike and – with the engine running, clutch in, and first gear selected – poke the stand down with your foot: if the engine stops, all is well. There's another safety cut-out to check; you should be able to start the engine with the stand down, but pull the clutch in and put the bike into first gear, and the engine should stop.

Electrics/wiring

All CBRs have fine electrics with a good charging system, lights, and accessories. But, as with anything else, they are vulnerable to neglect and enthusiastic amateurs. Look for clumsily spliced wires, flapping insulation tape, and crimp-on (not properly

Sounds obvious, but do the headlights work?

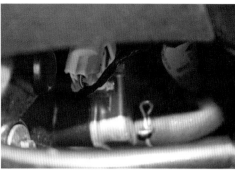

Look for signs of bodged wiring.

HISS immobiliser (1999-on) works well, but check the bike has a spare ignition key.

Rectifier/regulator lives under the right-hand side panel on carburettor bikes.

soldered) connectors. An alarm is the most common accessory, so if the bike has one, ask who fitted it and check the wiring.

It sounds obvious, but do check that everything electrical works as it should – lights, indicators, horn, warning lights, digital dash (on the later bikes), and side stand cut-outs. Many owners are wary of electrical problems, which may be as simple as a loose connector, bad earth, or blown fuse, so if you're confident of curing a fault, it's a good bargaining counter.

In fact, one part of the electrics does make up one of the CBR's rare weaknesses. The regulator/rectifier can fail, allowing the alternator to over-charge the battery until that, in turn, fails. Unfortunately, there's no easy way of checking this. If the battery is dead and won't accept a charge, this could well be the reason, even if the seller insists that just the battery is at fault. Cheap batteries can actually cause this problem, damaging the rectifier so that the charge circuit is permanently on.

The bottom line is that if the bike starts promptly, then there should be nothing to worry about. If the battery is dead, you could be looking at a new rectifier (around ◍x75) as well as a new battery. The rectifier is easy to find on early bikes, under the right-hand side panel, towards the rear of the bike.

Worn tyres – this one's almost new – are a good bargaining point.

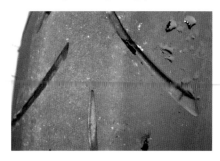

The examination needs to be up close.

Some CBRs are left sitting in the garage for long periods, especially over winter, so tired batteries aren't that uncommon. If the owner has hooked the battery up to a trickle charger while the bike is laid up, that's a good sign.

Wheels/tyres

All CBRs have cast alloy wheels and tubeless tyres. Tyre life varies widely according to riding style and, in any case, the CBR isn't as tyre hungry as a mega-powerful litre bike.

Take a good look at the tyres: if they're a well known top brand – Bridgestone, Avon, Metzeler etc – that's a good sign. If they have less than 50% of their tread left, then include the replacement cost in your negotiations. Check them for damage and sidewall cracks and look at the wear pattern. If they're worn right up to the sidewalls, that's another sign of a hard rider (not necessarily a bad thing, as long as they've cared for the bike). If the rear, in particular, is worn flat, it means the bike has done a lot of straight-line motorway miles, though you are less likely to encounter this. On an early bike with a narrow rear rim, check that an oversize tyre hasn't been fitted.

Now for the wheels. CBR600 Fs have a centre stand, which makes the next check a whole lot easier – on an RR or F-Sport with only a side stand, a paddock stand will do the same job. If the seller has a paddock stand, that's a good sign of a conscientious owner. If you don't have either, then prop the bike up with a car jack or (if you can do so safely and securely) a block of wood, though you'll need a helper to keep the bike steady. However you do it, prop up each end in turn and spin the wheel; it should run true, and there should be no dents or cracks in the rim.

Flaking rim paint does no harm, but looks unsightly.

Check the front wheel bearings for play ...

... and the rears.

While the bike's propped up, check the wheel bearings. These aren't expensive, but fitting them is a hassle, and if there's play it will affect the handling, so it's vital that they are in top condition. To check the front wheel, put the steering on full lock and try rocking the wheel in a vertical plane, then spin the wheel and listen for rumbles. Give the rear wheel the same rocking and rumbling checks.

It's not just mileage that can kill wheel bearings; wheelies give the front bearings a hard life, and over-zealous jet washing can force the grease out of bearings at either end.

Steering head bearings

Again, the bearings don't cost and arm or leg, but trouble here can affect the

handling, and changing them is a big job. Swing the handlebars from lock to lock. They should move freely, with no hint of roughness or stiff patches; if there is, budget for replacing them. To check for play, put the steering on full lock, grip the front wheel, and try rocking it back and forth. With the front wheel on the ground, apply the front brake and try to push bike forward; there should be no clonks (though this can be confused with fork wear – see below). Again, wheelies, beloved as they are by some CBR riders, put a lot of strain on steering head bearings.

Don't forget the steering head bearings.

Swing arm bearings

Another essential for good handling is the swing arm bearings. To check for wear,

prop up the rear of the bike, get hold of the rear end of the arm on one side, and try rocking the complete swing arm from side to side. There should be no perceptible movement: if there's any play in the bearings, then replacement is a dealer job.

Swing arm pivot bearings need checking, too.

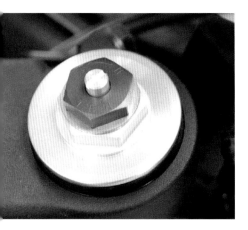

Fork adjusters shouldn't be 'butchered.'

Inverted forks were fitted from 2005.

Pump the forks up and down to check for wear.

Front forks 　4　3　2　1

All CBRs have adjustable telescopic front forks (upside-down types from 2005). The stanchions should be clean, and not pitted or rusted. Minor oil weeps aren't a problem, and major ones will be obvious. Replacement isn't a small job, so either negotiate the price down, or find another bike.

To check the forks for wear, first pump them up and down with the front brake on. They should move smoothly with no squeaks or clonks. Try pushing the bike back and forth with the front brake still on; any movement could be play in the forks or steering head bearings, and it's often difficult to tell which. Alternatively, with the front of the bike propped up, grasp the bottom of the forks and try rocking them back and forth. Again, it may not be obvious whether any movement is in the steering head or the forks themselves, but there should be no play in either.

Well worn forks are a sign of very high mileage or a wheelie-loving rider, ditto the fork seals. But the seals can last 90,000 miles if the bike has had regular rinsings to get rid of winter salt and grit.

CBR forks are multi-adjustable for pre-load and damping, and how they feel will depend on the seller's preference (though some owners never touch the adjusters). If the pre-load is set correctly, the forks should sink by 20mm when the bike is eased off the centre stand. Check that the pre-load adjusters (on top of the forks) haven't been butchered by a ham-fisted owner.

Rear shock is best checked on the test ride.

Rear suspension

To test the single rear shock, bounce up and down on the seat: the movement should be fairly stiff and well controlled. Out on the test ride, if the rear end feels oversoft and bouncy, then the bike probably needs a new shock, which won't be cheap. Early rear shocks could lose their damping control or even seize, though most will have been replaced by now. If there is a problem, it shows up in a rock hard ride, or no damping at all, which gives a bouncy ride over bumps.

Visually check the shock, the pressure canister, and its hose for leaks. Ensure the shock is firmly mounted, and that the linkage moves freely. The linkage can stiffen if left dirty and unused for long periods. The same goes for the pre-load adjustment collar – it's surprising how many riders leave this on the same setting, regardless of whether they're carrying a passenger, or the type of riding they're doing.

Matching speedo and rev counter on earlier machines.

Instruments

Fuel-injected bikes have a digital/ analogue display.

Carburettor bikes had analogue instruments, fuel-injected bikes (2001 onwards) a digital set, with a speedometer, rev counter and temp gauge. It's a case of waiting for the test ride to check that they are all working, and – in nearly every case – the drive is electronic. Early speedos were cable drive; if neither speedometer nor mileometer work, then the cable or drive gearbox is at fault. If one or the other works, then the speedo itself needs work.

If the bike has a coolant temperature gauge, keep an eye on it during the test ride; it shouldn't reach more than halfway around the dial.

Engine/gearbox – general impression

Hondas have a good reputation for mechanical reliability, and deservedly so. The CBR600 is no exception, with a strong, robust engine/gearbox that only really gives

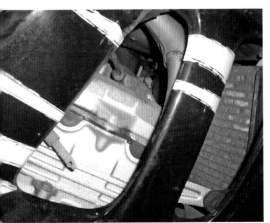

trouble if abused or neglected. Some of the bikes pictured in this book have covered over 60,000 miles without any major problems, and there are even a few 100,000-milers out there.

At first glance, both engine and gearbox appear to be completely hidden by the fairing, and whether you can remove the lower panels is up to the seller. But, even if they're unwilling, you can still ascertain a lot from the outside. If any fastenings (and this applies

You can't see much of the engine, but do check for leaks.

to every component on the bike) are rounded-off or generally butchered, that's a bad sign. Ideally, the bike will have a full service history (with oil/filter changes every 4000 miles).

A good indicator of whether a bike has been cared for is the condition of the engine oil. To check this, the bike should be warm and left for a couple of minutes after switching off, to allow the oil to drain back into the sump. Early bikes have a screw-in filler cap/dipstick, on the right-hand side. With the bike upright, unscrew the cap then place it back in, lightly, without screwing it in: the oil should be between the lower and upper marks. Later CBRs have a sight glass in the bottom of the crankcase – easier to check if an assistant holds the bike vertical, while you check that the oil level is between the two marks. In either case, the oil should be brown in colour: if it's black, or smells burned, or – worse still – has visible particles floating in it, then the engine has serious internal problems. Of course, it could be that the oil simply hasn't been changed in a very long time, but that in itself is a bad sign.

However much of the engine you can see, make a visual check for oil leaks, and of the coolant hoses and pump for coolant leaks. None are likely, but it's worth checking. Water pumps can fail by 50,000 miles, but some bikes cover far more miles with no problems at all. If the pump has failed, then it will be immediately obvious by rapid overheating. Have a look underneath at the sump plate, which could have been damaged by a jack, or the bike hitting a kerb.

Engine – starting/idling

[4] [3] [2] [1]

The engine should start promptly on the button; if the starter is sluggish, then a tired

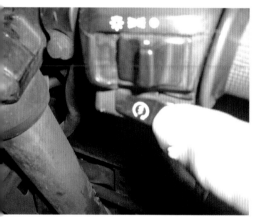

Engine should fire up promptly.

battery is the most likely cause. The starter motor itself isn't noted for problems, though, if it does wear out, it'll cost more to put right than a duff battery. Remember that carburettor bikes (pre-2001) have a manual choke.

Whether it's carb or fuel-injection, once started the engine should settle down to a steady idle of 1100-1200rpm. The fuel-injection system is extremely reliable, but if there's an idling fault with it, then it's a dealer job to fix. With the engine idling, push the bars slowly from lock to lock . If the engine speed rises or falls, then the throttle and/or choke cables are badly routed.

Difficulty starting and erratic running on carburettor bikes is often simply down to dirty carbs: if the bike has been unused for a long time, the fuel in the carbs evaporates, leaving gunge (there's no better word for it). The only cure is to remove the carburettors and clean them all out.

Failure to start on a 1999/2000 machine could have a very simple cause: an electrical connector near the seat rim can be come adrift when the seat is removed/replaced.

Not a CBR600, but if you see blue smoke
it's a sign of engine wear.

Engine – smoke/noise

With the engine warm, blip the throttle and watch for smoke. White smoke is harmless – just water vapour escaping as the engine warms up. Black smoke is due to an over-rich fuel/air mixture, the most likely cause on carburettor bikes (aside from a blocked air filter) being a carb incorrectly jetted to suit an aftermarket air cleaner and/or exhaust. Blue smoke is more serious; the engine is burning oil, which is down to straightforward wear at the top end. You're unlikely to come across this, unless the engine has covered 50,000 miles or more.

Listen to the engine: all CBR600 power units are water-cooled, and should be relatively quiet, mechanically. If the CBR has an engine weakness, it's the camchain tensioner.

As with any chain-driven overhead cam engine, the cam chain and its tensioner are vital to the engine's health. It's unusual for the tensioner to break, but it can happen, in which case the chain rattle will be obvious at idle. On the other hand, a rattle could just meant that dirt has worked its way into the tensioner valve, preventing it from keeping the chain at its correct tension. The cure is to take the tensioner out and clean it with brake cleaner. Apart from listening for rattles, the only way to check the chain tension is to take the cam cover off and push the chain down between the two cam sprockets; the chain should not sag more than 3mm. A few bikes have been fitted with an aftermarket manual camchain adjuster, so ask if this has been done – if so, adjustment becomes part of the maintenance schedule.

A knocking at half engine speed suggests worn camshaft lobes or followers, though this is something that will only come up if oil changes have been neglected. At the bottom of the engine, listen for rumblings (crankshaft main bearings) or knocks (big-ends) – again, it could be tardy oil changes, and either way, reason enough to reject the bike altogether, unless it's a real bargain.

While the engine is running, pull the clutch lever in. If it's noisy, then the springs are likely to be worn out. If the engine has been tuned, then the clutch will have had a particularly hard time. But don't let any of this put you off: the CBR engine is a tough one, and serious problems are rare.

Main warning lights

Check that all the warning lights work – indicators, main beam, side stand, oil pressure, water temp – the exact array depends on which bike you are looking at.

If any lights fail to come on with the ignition, an unscrupulous owner might have actually removed the bulb to hide a more serious problem.

The oil light should go out the second the engine fires up – if it doesn't, there's serious engine wear or oil/filter changes have been neglected. It may simply be down to a faulty sender unit, but suspect the worst. If it comes on during hard acceleration, the oil level is probably low (not a sign of a caring owner).

Do the warning lights work? Don't forget side stand, HISS and ABS warning lights.

1999-on bikes come with Honda's HISS immobiliser system. The red HISS warning light should go out a few seconds after the ignition is switched on. If it stays on, on a fuel-injected bike, the cam pulse generators (that tell the ECU where the crank is) may be at fault. If the bike won't start and the HISS light stays on, then they've almost certainly failed. One other point about HISS: make sure the bike comes with its spare ignition key, as a replacement set is expensive.

Chain/sprockets

With the engine switched off, examine the final drive chain and rear sprocket (the front sprocket is hidden). Is the chain clean, well lubed and properly adjusted? The best way to check how worn it is, is to take hold of a link and try to pull it rearwards, away from the sprocket. It should reveal only a small portion of the sprocket teeth – any more, and it needs replacing.

Examine the rear sprocket for signs of wear.

A well lubed and adjusted chain is a sign of a caring owner.

Check the rear sprocket teeth for wear; if they have a hooked appearance, the sprocket needs replacing. Ditto if any teeth are missing or damaged. And, if the rear sprocket needs replacing, then the front (which is smaller and spins faster, so therefore wears out more quickly) certainly will. The chain and sprockets aren't particularly expensive, but changing the front sprocket takes some dismantling time.

Exhaust

An aftermarket silencer is probably the most common CBR modification, especially

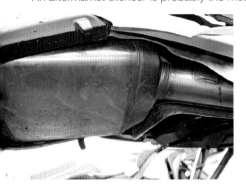

Underseat silencer on RR.

on early bikes, whose mild steel can lose its paint and, eventually, rust from the inside (although they do last reasonably well). Later bikes have aluminium alloy or (best of all for a longevity) stainless steel silencers. If there is a non-standard silencer, check that it's road legal (it might be stamped 'not for road use') and, on the test ride, power delivery. On fuel-injected CBRs, an aftermarket exhaust can actually reduce power slightly if the injection isn't remapped to suit. If the bike comes with its original can as well, so much the better.

Early original steel silencer can last well.

The downpipes are mostly visible, so have a good look. Light surface rust is no problem, but there shouldn't be any holes or leaks. High mileage bikes may have cracks, especially on the central fixing lug.

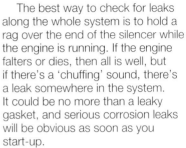

The best way to check for leaks along the whole system is to hold a rag over the end of the silencer while the engine is running. If the engine falters or dies, then all is well, but if there's a 'chuffing' sound, there's a leak somewhere in the system. It could be no more than a leaky gasket, and serious corrosion leaks will be obvious as soon as you start-up.

Cables (clutch, throttle, choke) should work smoothly.

Cables

The control cables – clutch, throttle and (on carburettor bikes) choke – should work smoothly, without stiffness or jerking. Poorly lubricated, badly adjusted cables are an indication of general neglect, and the same goes for badly routed cables.

Switchgear

The switchgear is straightforward and reliable, with no particular faults. Check that everything works, and, if it doesn't, the cure could be fairly simple. As mentioned, many owners are wary of electrical faults, but if you're confident of putting it right, this could be a good lever on the price.

Brakes

CBR brakes improved greatly over the years, from early 2-pot calipers (not that good by modern standards), to far more powerful 4-pot calipers from the FireBlade (later radially mounted) and, finally, to an optional linked ABS system. Whatever the system, the check points are the same.

Have a close look at the discs: are they thin, or badly scored? Discs can also warp if the bike is used hard. They can also crack between the holes drilled in the disc, especially between the hole and the disc rim. Try pushing the bike forwards a few feet; it should

Switchgear is reliable.

run freely, but if the brakes are binding, the disc could be warped, or the calipers sticking. The latter can happen if the calipers aren't cleaned regularly, particularly on bikes used year round, or put away for the winter without being cleaned. Braided hoses are a good sign.

ABS was optional from 2009. It's a complex system that works very well and has

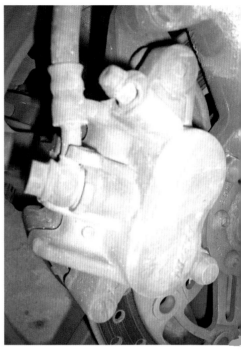

Any caliper can stick if left unused for long periods.

Late model radial-mount caliper is very powerful.

no particular faults. Look out for ABS badging and the small serrated ring on the front hub. The ABS warning light should go out once the bike reaches 10mph.

Test ride ④ ③ ② ①

The test ride should not be less than 10 minutes, and you should be doing the riding – not the seller riding with you on the pillion. It's understandable that some sellers are reluctant to let a complete

Check discs for cracks, scoring, and thickness.

stranger loose on their pride and joy, but it does go with the territory of selling a bike, and so long as you leave an article of faith (usually the vehicle you arrived in), then all should be happy. Take your driving licence in case the seller wants to see it.

The bike should start promptly, after which you should allow a short while to familiarise yourself with the controls (and the riding position, if this is the first sports bike you've ridden). Tug the levers, and blip the throttle to get a feel for it. Check that the oil light has gone out, select first gear (which should click in easily), and set off. Clutch take-up should be smooth and progressive.

The CBR doesn't have a lot of low speed torque, but in that respect it's little different to any other 600cc sports bike. But it should still pull smoothly from low revs without hesitation or hiccups. If it falters (and this is true right through the rev range), the bike probably hasn't been set up properly for a non-standard exhaust. If the silencer is standard, then it's likely the owner has refitted it, but not bothered to re-jet the carbs or remap the injection system.

Over 5000rpm (and especially over 8-9000rpm) any CBR in good condition should accelerate very rapidly. Don't abuse the bike, but, if it's safe (and you will need a clear road), take it up to the red line once, in a low gear: the engine should rev freely, with vivid acceleration. If you've never ridden a bike with this power before, it's a good idea to bring an experienced friend along to do the test ride.

Older bikes have a fairly clunky, long travel gearshift, which needs a firm foot,

A test ride is crucial.

but this is normal. Ditto transmission lash at low revs. The important thing is that the bike doesn't jump out of gear, either under acceleration or on the overrun – if it does, you could be looking at a costly stripdown to put it right. Watch for clutch slip as you accelerate hard, and if the bike jumps forward when you click into first, the clutch is dragging: it shouldn't do either.

CBR's handle very well, and even with worn forks and rear shock, they shouldn't be too wayward. If it doesn't feel right, then the most likely causes are worn tyres or steering head bearings (both easy to check). Of course, it could be down to crash damage and a bent frame. If in doubt, look for another machine. If the bike wallows and feels underdamped (or, for that matter, too stiff) this could just be a case of suspension adjustment. Both the forks and the rear shock are multi-adjustable, so ask the owner how they have it set up. A track day addict, for example, will have much more pre-load than is needed on the road. The brakes should pull the bike up smoothly and progressively, without pulling to one side.

Back at base, check that the engine settles back into a nice, steady idle before switching off. If all is well, talk to the owner about price. If you've discovered a fault, and he/she won't make a deal, then thank them for their time and walk away.

Evaluation procedure
Add up the total points.
Score: 100 = excellent; 75 = good; 50 = average; 25 = poor.

Bikes scoring over 70 will be completely usable and will require only maintenance and care to preserve condition. Bikes scoring between 25 and 51 will require some serious work (at much the same cost regardless of score). Bikes scoring between 52 and 69 will require very careful assessment of necessary repair/restoration costs in order to arrive at a realistic value.

10 Auctions
– sold! Another way to buy your dream

Auction pros & cons

Pros: Prices will usually be lower than those of dealers or private sellers and you might grab a real bargain on the day. Auctioneers have usually established clear title with the seller. At the venue you can usually examine documentation relating to the bike.

Cons: You have to rely on a sketchy catalogue description of condition and history. The opportunity to inspect is limited and you cannot ride the bike. Auction machines can be a little below par and may require some work. It's easy to overbid. There will usually be a buyer's premium to pay in addition to the auction hammer price.

Which auction?

Auctions by established auctioneers are advertised in the motorcycle magazines and on the auction houses' websites. A catalogue, or a simple printed list of the lots for auction, might only be available a day or two ahead, though often lots are listed and pictured on auctioneers' websites much earlier. Contact the auction company to ask if previous auction selling prices are available as this is useful information (details of past sales are often available on websites).

Catalogue, entry fee and payment details

When you purchase the catalogue of the bikes in the auction, it often acts as a ticket allowing two people to attend the viewing days and the auction. Catalogue details tend to be comparatively brief, but will include information such as 'one owner from new, low mileage, full service history,' etc. It will also usually show a guide price to give you some idea of what to expect to pay and will tell you what is charged as a 'Buyer's premium.' The catalogue will also contain details of acceptable forms of payment. At the fall of the hammer an immediate deposit is usually required, the balance payable within 24 hours. If the plan is to pay by cash there may be a cash limit. Some auctions will accept payment by debit card. Sometimes credit or charge cards are acceptable, but will often incur an extra charge. A bank draft or bank transfer will have to be arranged in advance with your own bank as well as with the auction house. No bike will be released before all payments are cleared. If delays occur in payment transfers then storage costs can accrue.

Buyer's premium

A buyer's premium will be added to the hammer price: don't forget this in your calculations. It is not unusual for there to be a further state tax or local tax on the purchase price and/or on the buyer's premium.

Viewing

In some instances it's possible to view on the day, or days before, as well as in the hours prior to, the auction. There are auction officials available who are willing to help out if need be. While the officials may start the engine for you, a test ride is out of the question. Crawling under and around the bike as much as you want is permitted. You can also ask to see any documentation available.

Bidding

Before you take part in the auction, decide your maximum bid – and stick to it!

It may take a while for the auctioneer to reach the lot you are interested in, so use that time to observe how other bidders behave. When it's the turn of your bike, attract the auctioneer's attention and make an early bid. The auctioneer will then look to you for a reaction every time another bid is made, usually the bids will be in fixed increments until the bidding slows, when smaller increments will often be accepted before the hammer falls. If you want to withdraw from the bidding, make sure the auctioneer understands your intentions – a vigorous shake of the head when he or she looks to you for the next bid should do the trick!

Assuming that you are the successful bidder, the auctioneer will note your card or paddle number, and from that moment on you will be responsible for the bike.

If it is unsold, either because it failed to reach the reserve or because there was little interest, it may be possible to negotiate with the owner, via the auctioneers, after the sale is over.

Successful bid

There are two more items to think about – how to get the bike home, and insurance. If you can't ride it, your own or a hired trailer or van is one way, another is to have it shipped using the facilities of a local company. The auction house will also have details of companies specialising in the transport of bikes.

Insurance for immediate cover can usually be purchased on site, but it may be more cost-effective to make arrangements with your own insurance company in advance, and then call to confirm the full details.

eBay & other online auctions?

eBay & other online auctions could land you a CBR at a bargain price, though you'd be foolhardy to bid without examining it first, something most vendors encourage. A useful feature of eBay is that the geographical location of the bike is shown, so you can narrow your choices to those within a realistic radius of home. Be prepared to be outbid in the last few moments of the auction. Remember, your bid is binding and that it will be very, very difficult to get restitution in the case of a crooked vendor fleecing you – caveat emptor!

Be aware that some bikes offered for sale in online auctions are 'ghost' machines. Don't part with any cash without being sure that the vehicle does actually exist and is as described (usually pre-bidding inspection is possible).

Auctioneers

Bonhams www.bonhams.com
British Car Auctions (BCA)
www.bca-europe.com or
www.british-car-auctions.co.uk
Cheffins www.cheffins.co.uk
Dorset Vintage and Classic Auctions
www.dvca.co.uk

eBay www.eBay.com
H&H www.classic-auctions.co.uk
Palmer Snell www.palmersnell.co.uk
Shannons www.shannons.com.au
Silver www.silverauctions.com

11 Paperwork
– correct documentation is essential!

The paper trail
Pre-owned bikes sometimes come with a large portfolio of paperwork accumulated and passed on by a succession of proud owners. This documentation represents a real history of the machine, from which you can deduce how well it's been cared for, how much it's been used, which dealers or specialists have worked on it and the dates of major repairs and servicing. All of this information will be priceless to you as the new owner, so be very wary of bikes with little paperwork to support their claimed history.

Registration documents
All countries/states have some form of registration for private vehicles whether it's like the American 'pink slip' system or the British 'log book' system.

It is essential to check that the registration document is genuine, that it relates to the bike in question, and that all the details are correctly recorded, including frame and engine numbers (if these are shown). If you are buying from the previous owner, his or her name and address will be recorded in the document: this will not be the case if you are buying from a dealer.

In the UK the current (Euro-aligned) registration document is the V5C, and is printed in coloured sections of blue, green and pink. The blue section relates to the motorcycle specification, the green section has details of the registered keeper (who is not necessarily the legal owner) and the pink section is sent to the DVLA in the UK when the bike is sold. A small section in yellow deals with selling within the motor trade.

In the UK the DVLA will provide details of earlier keepers of the bike upon payment of a small fee, and much can be learned in this way.

When buying a rare bike, it's sometimes worth actually locating one overseas and importing it – not the case with CBR600s, of which thousands exist in all the major markets.

Bear in mind that the bike may be a 'parallel import.' This affected some markets (especially the UK) in the 1990s, when official UK prices were higher than those in some other European countries, so some non-UK specification machines were imported unofficially. These are not inferior to an officially imported bike, but most buyers prefer a genuine UK-spec machine.

Roadworthiness certificate
Most country/state administrations require that bikes are regularly tested to prove that they are safe to use on the public highway. In the UK that test (the 'MoT') is carried out at approved testing stations, for a fee. In the USA the requirement varies, but most states insist on an emissions test every two years as a minimum, while the police are charged with pulling over unsafe-looking vehicles.

In the UK the test is required on an annual basis once a vehicle becomes three years old. Of particular relevance for older bikes is that the certificate issued includes the mileage reading recorded at the test date and, therefore, becomes an independent record of that machine's history. Ask the seller if previous certificates are available. Without an MoT the vehicle should be trailered to its new home, unless you insist that a valid MoT is part of the deal. (Not such a bad idea this, as at least you will know the bike was roadworthy on the day it was tested and you don't need to wait for the old certificate to expire before having the test done.)

Road licence
The administration of every country/state charges some kind of tax for the use of its road system, the actual form of the 'road licence' and, how it is displayed, varying enormously country to country and state to state.

Whatever the form of the road licence, it must relate to the vehicle carrying it and must be present and valid if the bike is to be ridden on the public highway legally. The value of the license will depend on the length of time it will continue to be valid.

In the UK if a bike is untaxed because it has not been used for a period of time, the owner has to inform the licencing authorities, otherwise the vehicle's date-related registration number will be lost and there will be a painful amount of paperwork to get it re-registered.

Service history
A service history is a valuable record, and the more of it there is, the better. The ultimate consists of every single routine service bill (from an official Honda dealer, or a known and respected independent), plus bills for all other repairs and accessories.

But really, anything helps in the great authenticity game, items like the original bill of sale, handbook, parts invoices and those repair bills, all adding to the story and the character of the machine. Even a brochure correct to the year of the bike's manufacture is a useful document and something that you could well have to search hard to locate in future years. If the seller claims that the bike has been restored, then expect receipts and other evidence from a specialist restorer.

If the bike has only patchy or non-existent service history, then it could still be perfectly good, but the lack of history should be reflected in the price.

Restoration photographs
If the seller tells you that the bike has been restored, then expect to be shown a series of photographs taken while the restoration was under way. Pictures taken at various stages, and from various angles, should help you gauge the thoroughness of the work. If you buy the bike, ask if you can have all the photographs, as they form an important part of its history. It's surprising how many sellers are happy to part with their bike and accept your cash, but want to hang on to their photographs! In the latter event, you may be able to persuade the vendor to get a set of copies made.

12 What's it worth?

– let your head rule your heart

Condition

If the bike you've been looking at is really ratty, then you've probably not bothered to use the marking system in chapter 9. You may not have even got as far as using that chapter at all!

If you did use the marking system in chapter 9, you'll know whether the bike is in Excellent (maybe Concours), Good, Average or Poor condition or, perhaps, somewhere in between these categories.

To keep up to date with prices, buy the latest editions of the bike magazines (also *Bike Trader* and *MCN* in the UK) and check the classified and dealer ads – these are particularly useful as they enable you to compare private and dealer prices. Some of the magazines run auction reports too, publishing the actual selling prices, as do the auction house websites. Most of the dealers will have up to date websites as well.

CBR600 values in general are still falling, simply because these are modern bikes that sold in big numbers. The earliest bikes in good original condition are unlikely to get much cheaper now but, otherwise, all CBRs are depreciating. In that, they're no different to any other modern bike, and should offer you a good portion of fun per pound/dollar.

Assuming that the bike you have in mind is not in show/concours condition, then relate the level of condition that you judge it to be in with the appropriate price in the adverts. How does the figure compare with the asking price?

Absolute originality isn't a big deal, and, in any case, the most common accessories can, quite easily, be unbolted and replaced with standard parts. That's if you can find the standard parts at an affordable price.

If you are buying from a dealer, remember there will be a dealer's premium on the price.

Striking a deal

Negotiate on the basis of your condition assessment, mileage, and fault rectification cost. Also take into account the bike's specification. Be realistic about the value, but don't be completely intractable: a small compromise on the part of the vendor or buyer will often facilitate a deal at little real cost.

13 Do you really want to restore?
– it'll take longer and cost more than you think

'Quick' restorations can be a tempting prospect; the promise of a bike that 'just needs a few small jobs' to bring it up to scratch. But, there are two things to think about: first, once you've got the bike home and start taking it apart, those few small jobs could turn into big ones. Second, restoration takes time, which is a precious thing in itself. Be honest with yourself: will you get as much pleasure from working on the bike as you will from riding it?

Flaking paint is easy to rectify.

This applies to restoring any bike, but in the case of the CBR600, you need to think harder still. The fact is that Honda's 600 is too numerous and not yet old enough to be classed an investment. The CBR is well loved and respected by thousands of riders, but that hasn't yet translated into soaring values. So, if you do buy something tatty, and spend time and money restoring it, it's unlikely to bag you a profit.

Still, there are always exceptions, so let's assume that you've found a bike, maybe at a bargain price, that needs a great deal of work to get it back on the road. You could hand the whole job over to a professional, and the biggest cost involved there is not the new parts, but the sheer labour involved. Such restorations don't come cheap, and if taking this route there are four other issues to bear in mind as well.

First, make it absolutely clear what you want doing. Do you want the bike to be 100% original at the end of the process, or simply useable? Do you want a concours finish, or are you prepared to put up with a few blemishes on the original parts?

Second, make sure that a detailed estimate involved, and that it is, more or less, binding. There are too many stories of a person being quoted a figure, only to be presented with an invoice for a far larger one!

Third, check that the company you're dealing with has a good reputation. The owners' club, or one of the reputable parts suppliers, should be able to make a few recommendations.

Finally, the restoration cost will never be recouped when you come to sell the bike – with a Vincent Black Lightning, perhaps, but not with a Honda CBR600!

Restoring a CBR yourself requires a number of skills: fine if you already have

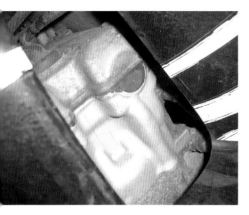

Corroded alloy is a cosmetic problem only.

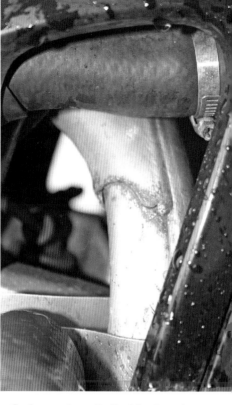

Surface rust won't affect the frame's integrity. Do you really want a concours finish?

them, but if you haven't, it's best not to make your newly acquired bike part of the learning curve! Can you weld? Are you confident about building up an engine? Do you have a warm, well-lit garage with a solid workbench and a good selection of tools?

Be prepared for a top-notch professional to put you on a lengthy waiting list, or, if tackling a restoration yourself, expect things to go wrong and set aside extra time to complete the task. Restorations can stretch into years when things like life intrude, so it's good to have some idea of a target date.

A rolling restoration is tempting, especially as the summer begins to pass with your bike still off the road. This is not the way to achieve a concours finish, which can only really be done via a thorough nut-and-bolt rebuild, without the bike getting wet and dirty in the meantime. But there's a lot to be said for a rolling restoration. Riding the bike helps maintain your interest as its condition improves, and it's also more affordable than trying to do everything in one go. It will take longer, but you'll get some on-road fun in the meantime.

14 Paint problems
– bad complexion, including dimples, pimples and bubbles

Paint faults generally occur due to lack of protection/maintenance, or to poor preparation prior to a respray or touch-up. Some of the following conditions may be present in the bike you're looking at:

A cutting compound should remove marks like these.

Orange peel
This appears as an uneven paint surface, similar to the appearance of the skin of an orange. The fault is caused by the failure of atomised paint droplets to flow into each other when they hit the surface. It's sometimes possible to rub out the effect with proprietary paint cutting/rubbing compound or very fine grades of abrasive paper. A respray may be necessary in severe cases. Consult a paint shop for advice.

Cracking
Severe cases are likely to have been caused by too heavy an application of paint (or filler beneath the paint). Also, insufficient stirring of the paint before application can lead to the components being improperly mixed, and cracking can result. Incompatibility with the paint already on the panel can have a similar effect. To rectify it is necessary to rub down to a smooth, sound finish before respraying the problem area.

Crazing
Sometimes the paint takes on a crazed rather than a cracked appearance when the problems mentioned under 'cracking' are present. This problem can also be caused

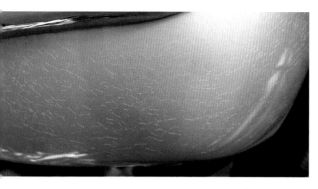

A respray is the only cure for crazing.

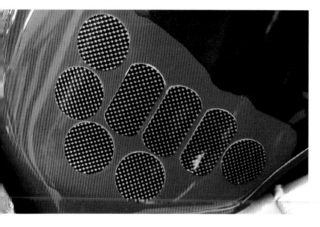

Carbon-look stickers are often used to protect the tank's paintwork.

by a reaction between the underlying surface and the paint. Paint removal and respraying the problem area is usually the only solution.

Blistering

Almost always caused by corrosion of the metal beneath the paint. Usually perforation will be found in the metal and the damage will usually be worse than that suggested by the area of blistering. The metal will have to be repaired before repainting.

Micro blistering

Usually the result of an economy respray where inadequate heating has allowed moisture to settle on the vehicle before spraying. Consult a paint specialist, but damaged paint will have to be removed before partial or full respraying. Can also be caused by bike covers that don't 'breathe.'

Fading

Some colours, especially reds, are prone to fading if subjected to strong sunlight for long periods without the benefit of polish protection. Sometimes proprietary paint restorers and/or paint cutting/rubbing compounds will retrieve the situation. Often a respray is the only real solution.

Peeling

Often a problem with metallic paintwork when the sealing lacquer becomes damaged and begins to peel off. Poorly applied paint may also peel. The remedy is to strip and start again.

Dimples

Dimples in the paintwork are caused by the residue of polish (particularly silicone types) not being removed properly before respaying. Paint removal and repainting is the only solution.

15 Problems due to lack of use

– just like their owners, CBRs need exercise!

CBRs deteriorate if sat doing nothing for long periods, just like any other piece of engineering, or for that matter, human beings! This is especially relevant if the bike is laid up for the winter.

Rust
If the bike is put away wet, and/or stored in a cold, damp garage, the paint, metal, and alloy will suffer. Ensure the machine is completely dry and clean before going into storage, and if you can afford it, invest in a dehumidifier to keep the garage atmosphere dry.

Seized components
Pistons in brake calipers can seize partially or fully, resulting in binding or non-working brakes. Cables are vulnerable to seizure, too – the answer is to thoroughly lube them beforehand, and give them a couple of pulls once a week or so.

Tyres
When the bike is parked for long periods, most of its weight is on the tyres, which will subsequently develop flat spots and cracks over time. The only long-term answer is to put it up on blocks, or a paddock stand at each end.

Engine
Old, acidic oil can corrode bearings. Many riders change the oil in the spring when they're putting the bike back on the road, but really it should be changed just before the bike is laid up, so that the engine and gearbox bearings are sitting in fresh oil. Don't start the engine and run it for a short time – this simply produces condensation inside the engine that will lead to corrosion. Either give the bike a proper run of 10-20 miles, or leave it in peace.

Battery/electrics
Either remove the battery and give it a top-up charge every couple of weeks, or connect it to a battery top-up device such as the Optimate, which will keep it permanently fully charged. Damp conditions will allow fuses and earth connections to corrode, storing up electrical troubles for the spring. Eventually, wiring insulation will harden and fail.

Auctioneers

Bonhams
www.bonhams.com/

British Car Auctions BCA)
www.bca-europe.com
or www.british-car-auctions.co.uk

Cheffins
www.cheffins.co.uk/

Dorset Vintage and Classic Auctions
www.dvca.co.uk

eBay
www.eBay.com/

H&H
www.classic-auctions.co.uk/

Palmer Snell
www.palmersnell.co.uk

Shannons
www.shannons.com.au/

Silver
www.silverauctions.com

Useful websites and clubs across the world

Honda official website
www.world.honda.com/motorcycle
National sites for many countries on all
continents, including the USA, France,
Australia, Germany, France, Italy, Spain,
UK, Sweden, Netherlands etc

Honda sports bikes official site
www.powersports.honda.com/
motorcycles/sport

UK official site
www.honda.co.uk/motorcycles

Honda Owners club – UK
www.hoc.org.uk
The original Honda club, 50 years old in
2011.

Honda Riders Club of America
www.hrca.honda.com
The official USA club

Honda Club – Germany
www.hondaclub-germany.de
Honda club of Germany

Honda Riders Association – Belgium/Holland
www.hra.be
Honda club serving Holland and
Belgium

Website – Italy
www.cbr600-italia.it

Enthusiast Websites/Forums
www.cbr-forum.org.uk
www.cbrfan.com
www.bikersoracle.com/cbr600/forum

Spares specialists
All official Honda dealers supply
parts for the CBR600. For cheaper
secondhand parts, try a local bike
breaker. Other than that, there are few
independent shops that specialise
in Honda or CBR parts, below are a
couple in the UK. Routine service items
can also be sourced from any of the
online mail order suppliers.

David Silver Spares
www.davidsilverspares.co.uk
01728 833020

Lings Honda
www.hondaoriginalparts.com

17 Vital statistics
– essential data at your fingertips

To list the specification of every CBR600 would take more room than we have here, so we've picked three representative models:

Max speed
1987 CBR600 F – 140mph
2001 CBR600 F-Sport – 155mph
2010 CBR600 RR – 165mph

Engine
1987 CBR600 F – Liquid-cooled DOHC in-line four, 599cc, 4 x carbs, Bore and stroke 63 x 48mm. Compression ratio 11:1. 83bhp @11,000rpm, 6-speed gearbox
2001 CBR600 F-Sport – Liquid-cooled DOHC in-line four, 599cc, electronic fuel-injection, Bore and stroke 57 x 42.5mm. 109bhp @ 12,500rpm, 6-speed gearbox
2010 CBR600 RR – Liquid-cooled DOHC in-line four, 599cc, PGM-DFSI fuel-injection, Bore and stroke 67 x 42.5mm, Compression ratio 12.2:1, 120bhp @ 13,500rpm, 6-speed gearbox

Final drive
1987 CBR600 F – Exposed chain
2001 CBR600 F-Sport – Exposed chain
2010 CBR600 RR – Exposed chain

Suspension
1987 CBR600 F – F: 41mm forks, preload/rebound adj. R: Monoshock, preload adj
2001 CBR600 F-Sport – F: 43mm forks, preload, rebound and compression adj R: Monoshock, preload, compression and rebound adj.
2010 RR-A – F: 41mm inverted HMAS cartridge forks. Preload, rebound and compression adj R: Unit Pro-Link monoshock. Preload, rebound and compression adj.

Brakes
1987 CBR600 F – F: 2 x 276mm discs, 2-pot calipers, R: 1 x 220mm disc, 1-pot caliper
2001 CBR600 F-Sport – F: 2 x 296 mm discs, 4-pot calipers, R: 1 x 220mm disc, 2-pot caliper
2010 CBR600 RR – F: 2 x 310mm discs, 4-pot radial calipers, R: 1 x 220mm disc, 2-pot caliper. Combined ABS system optional

Tyres
1987 CBR600 F – F: 110/80 ZR17 R: 130/80 ZR17
2001 CBR600 F-Sport – F: 120/70 ZR17 R: 180/55 ZR17
2010 CBR600 RR – F: 120/70 ZR17 R: 180/55 ZR17

Weight (kerb)
1992 RR-N – 182kg (dry)
1998 RR-W – 169kg (dry)
2010 RR-A – 184kg (kerb)

Major changes by year
1987   FH, 83bhp; CBR600 launched, steel frame, 140mph top speed
1988   FJ, 83bhp; No major changes
1989   FK, 93bhp; Higher power thanks to higher compression etc, 145mph, rebound damping adjustment for rear shock, uprated brakes, CBR badge on tank
1990   FL, 93bhp; No major changes
1991   FM, 99bhp; Shorter stroke engine with more power, 4-2-1 exhaust, higher seat, lower fairing, six-spoke wheels
1992   FN, 99bhp; No major changes
1993   FP, 99bhp; Stepless rebound damping adjustment on forks, compression damping adjustment on rear shock
1994   FR, 99bhp; No major changes
1995   FS, 100bhp; Ram air injection, higher compression, 36mm carbs
1996   FT, 100bhp; No major changes
1997   FV, 105bhp; CBR badge on bellypan
1998   FW, 105bhp; Engine/gearbox modifications
1999   FX, 110bhp; Alloy frame, all-new engine, 43mm forks, HISS immobiliser,
2000   FY, 110bhp; No major changes
2001   F1, 109bhp; FS-1 110bhp; F-Sport launched, similar to F but with two-piece seat, no centre stand, revised engine internals, 1kg lighter. Fuel-injection on both models, 160-165mph top speed
2002   F2, 111bhp; FS-2 111bhp; No major changes
2003   F3, 110bhp; FS-3 110bhp; RR-3 117bhp; RR launched to replace F-Sport, similar styling to RCV211V, Uni Pro Link rear end, lower bars, higher footrests, sharper geometry, 45mm forks, underseat exhaust
2004   F4 110bhp; RR-4 117bhp; No major changes
2005   F5, 110bhp; RR-5 117bhp; For RR, new bodywork, USD forks, radial-mounted brake calipers
2006   F6, 110bhp; RR-6 118bhp; No major changes
2007   RR-7 118bhp; Redesigned RR with new engine, frame and bodywork. Lighter, more compact bike.
2008   RR-8 118bhp; No major changes.
2009   RR-9 118bhp; Combined ABS braking available as option.
2010   RR-A 120bhp; No major changes

VIN number range (UK models)
Year	Model	Number Range
1987	FH	PC19200017 – 2008955
1988	FJ	PC192100101 – 2106485
1989	FK	PC232000144 – 2008231
1990	FL	PC232100659 – 2107310
1991	FM	PC25200059 – 2011020
1992	FN	PC252100030 – 2115605

1993	FP	PC252201237 – 2212108
1994	FR	PC252300751 – 2312384
1995	FS	PC312000062 – 2010685
1996	FT	JH2PC31A*TMTM00001 – TM006864
1997	FV	JH2PC31A*VMVM1000001 – VM104134
1998	FW	JH2PC34A*WMWM000001 – WM011815
1999	FX	JH2PC35A*XMXM000001 – XM099999
2000	FY	JH2PC35A*YMYM1000001 – YM199999
2001	F1	JH2PC35E*1M1M200001 – 1M299999
2001	FR1	JH2PC35G*1M1M250001 – 1M299999
2001	FS1	JH2PC35G*1M1M200001 – 1M249999
2002	F2	JH2PC359*2M2M300001 – 2M399999
2002	FR2	JH2PC35G*2M2M100001-2M319999
2002	FS2	JH2PC35G*2M2M300001 – 2M309999
2003	F3	JH2PC359*3M3M400001 – 3M499999
2003	RR3	JH2PC379*3M3M000001 – 3M099999
2004	F4	JH2PC35F*4M4M500001 – 4M509999
2004	RR4	JH2PC37B*4M4M100001 – 4M199999
2005	F5	JH2PC35F*5M5M600001 – 5M699999
2005	RR5	JH2PC379*5M5M200001 – 5M299999
2006	F6	JH2PC35F*6M6M700001 – 6M999999
2006	RR6	JH2PC37A*6M6M300001 – 6M399999
2007	RR7	JH2PC40A*7M7M000001 – 7M099999
2008	RR8	JH2PC40A*8K8K110001 – 8K119999
2009	RRA9	JH2PC40E*9K9K201448 – 9K299999 (ABS version)
2009	RR9	JH2PC40C*9K9K202514 – 9K299999 (MkVariant)
2009	RR9	JH2PC40C*2000001 – 9K202513 (MME variant)
2010	RAA	JH2PC40E*AKAK300001 – AK999999 (ABS version)
2010	RRA	JH2PC40C*AKAK300001 – AK999999

The **Essential** Buyer's Guide™ series

BUS	**TR6**	**MGB MGB GT**	**E-type**	**2CV**	**MINOR & 1000**	**280-560SL & SLC**
978-1-845840-22-8	978-1-845840-26-6	978-1-845840-29-7	978-1-845840-77-8	978-1-845840-99-0	978-1-845841-01-0	978-1-845841-07-2
230, 250 & 280SL	**XJ6, XJ12 & Sovereign**	**BONNEVILLE**	**GS**	**500 & 650 Twins**	**DS & ID**	**SILVER SHADOW & T-SERIES**
978-1-845841-13-3	978-1-845841-19-5	978-1-845841-34-8	978-1-845841-35-5	978-1-845841-36-2	978-1-845841-38-6	978-1-845841-46-1
500 & 600	**XJ-S**	**IMPREZA**	**Bantam**	**GOLF GTI**	**XJ40**	**XJ**
978-1-845841-47-8	978-1-845841-61-4	978-1-845841-63-8	978-1-845841-65-2	978-1-845841-88-1	978-1-845841-92-8	978-1-845842-00-0
MINI	**CAPRI**	**STAG**	**Commando**	**205 GTI**	**SOHC FOURS**	**TRIPLES & FOURS**
978-1-845842-04-8	978-1-845842-05-5	978-1-845842-70-3	978-1-845842-81-9	978-1-845842-83-3	978-1-845842-84-0	978-1-845842-87-1
Big Twins	**Fireblade**	**CBR600**	**TR7 & TR8**	**911sc**		**SCOOTERS**
978-1-845843-03-8	978-1-845843-07-6	978-1-845843-09-0	978-1-845843-16-8	978-1-845843-29-8	978-1-845843-30-4	978-1-845843-34-2
911 (964)	**911 (996)**	**911 (993)**	**SERIES I, II & IIA**	**TD TF & TF1500**	**SEVEN**	**MIDGET & SPRITE**
978-1-845843-38-0	978-1-845843-39-7	978-1-845843-40-3	978-1-845843-48-9	978-1-845843-52-6	978-1-845843-53-3	978-1-845843-54-0
Spitfire & GT6	**XK8**	**GT COUPÉ**	**928**	**BEETLE**		**SPIDER**
978-1-845843-56-4	978-1-845843-59-5	978-1-904788-69-0	978-1-904788-70-6	978-1-904788-72-0	978-1-904788-85-0	978-1-904788-98-0

£9.99*/$19.95*

*prices subject to change, p&p extra.
For more details visit www.veloce.co.uk or email info@veloce.co.uk

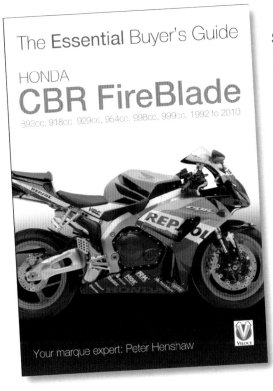

The Essential Buyer's Guide

HONDA
CBR FireBlade
893cc, 918cc, 929cc, 954cc, 998cc, 999cc, 1992 to 2010

REPSOL

HRC

REP*OL

Your marque expert: Peter Henshaw

STOP!
Don't buy a Honda
CBR Fireblade
without buying this
book first

• Paperback
• 19.5x13.9cm
• £9.99
• 64 pages
• 84 colour pictures
• ISBN: 978-1-845843-07-6

The FireBlade set new standards of sports bike performance and sold in big
numbers.

Really practical advice on what to look for when buying one secondhand.

Several books and many magazine articles have been written about the
FireBlade, but very little on buying one secondhand. This book fills the gap.

Also available from Veloce –

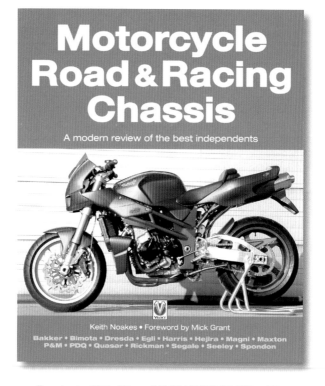

Motorcycle Road & Racing Chassis

A modern review of the best independents

Keith Noakes • Foreword by Mick Grant

Bakker • Bimota • Dresda • Egli • Harris • Hejira • Magni • Maxton
P&M • PDQ • Quasar • Rickman • Segale • Seeley • Spondon

• Paperback • 20.7 x 25cm • £19.99* UK/$39.95* USA • 176
pages • 246 colour and b&w pictures • ISBN: 978-1-845841-30-0

Cutting edge chassis design is a major factor in motorcycle performance.

This book charts the history of fifteen of the most innovative companies.

With full specifications for many chassis and extensively illustrated
throughout, this book is a must for any motorcycle enthusiast and a
valuable reference for the trade.

An account of the independent companies and individuals who have played a major part in the
design and advancement of motorcycle frame (chassis) performance. With full specifications
for many chassis and extensively illustrated throughout, this book is a must for any motorcycle
enthusiast, and a valuable reference for the trade.

Index